Merry Christmas

Farm Chicks Christmas Stickers

To help make your holidays merry, a page with decorative adhesive labels is bound into the back of the book. Some of them are specific to Christmas, some are timeless, many have space for a personal message, and all make it easy to add a festive touch to home-made baked goods or special gift wraps.

Here are some ideas for using the stickers:

★ Affix to a jar filled with small sweet treats or jam.

★ Use to seal an envelope that holds a special card.

★ Use to label a container filled with your favorite homemade cookies.

★ Affix to a gift box to hold a decorative ribbon in place.

★ Center on a gift tag cut from card stock; add a pretty string or ribbon so you can tie it to a gift.

★ Affix to the cover of a journal, book, or folder you've filled with your favorite recipes.

★ Use as a label on a box of craft supplies.

MERRY IDEAS *for the* HOLIDAYS

COUNTRY LIVING

THE ★ FARM CHICKS

Christmas

★ SERENA THOMPSON ★

HEARST BOOKS

A division of Sterling Publishing Co., Inc.

New York / London
www.sterlingpublishing.com

ACKNOWLEDGMENTS

Colin, Cody, Micah, Lucas, and Bongo: You're the greatest gift I could ever receive.

Teri: Some of my fondest memories are with you. Thank you for your friendship and the time we had together as business partners.

Celeste, Chris, Nancy, & Sally: Thank you for sharing your stories and beautiful homes.

John Granen: You made every picture sparkle.

Lana Lê: Thank you for designing and bringing this book to life.

Marisa Bulzone: I loved getting to work with you and miss you dearly.

Carol Spier: Thank you for your guidance. You're a joy.

Contents

Introduction

When I began thinking about a second Farm Chicks book, I knew it had to be all about Christmas, which for me is one of the best times of the year. I have a tendency to rearrange and redecorate my home on a regular basis, and Christmas provides the perfect opportunity to indulge this passion—I love the chance to unpack my favorite holiday collections and then decorate to my heart's content.

Christmas is also such a festive time, with all the baking, creating, decorating, and celebrating shared with friends and family, more than at any other time of the year. I love visiting my friends' homes and seeing the creativity with which they display their collections and decorate for the season. It's so inspiring. Three of my dearest friends, Teri—my original partner in the Farm Chicks, who is now retired, Nancy, and Celeste, all have magical holiday homes that you'll see sprinkled throughout this book. I hope you enjoy seeing their homes just as much as I have loved the time I've spent there. I invite you into my home and my friends' homes, and I hope you'll find inspiration to make your season merry and bright!

PART ONE

THE
Spirit
OF THE
Season

'Tis lovely to give

I've always been thankful I was raised in a family where expensive gifts weren't the focus of our Christmas, and I was greatly relieved to learn that Colin's family was the same way. In the first years of our marriage, sometime before the holidays each adult family member drew another's name and then gave that person a gift at Christmas, when we gathered at Grandpa Pete and Grandma Mary Jane's house. We do the kids' exchange differently, with each couple drawing names of two nieces or nephews.

Over the years, the gift exchange has evolved and, while we still give gifts to the children, we have stopped the adults' exchange altogether. We now all choose a charity and donate to that, rather than buy gifts for each other. It's been a really rewarding experience for our family, and a life lesson for our children. Some weeks, when shopping for groceries, I'll skip buying bread and prepare it from scratch instead. I talk with the boys about the savings from making homemade, and we add the saved money to the donation jar. They're always surprised to see how quickly the money from these practices can add up.

We all still enjoy gathering at Grandma and Grandpa's house on Christmas Day, watching the kids open their exchange gifts, sledding, and snacking. And we're so thankful that we've been able to give rather than receive.

MY CHILDHOOD CHRISTMAS
Christmas was always a really big deal in my childhood home, but in a very simple sort of way. Since we owned forty heavily timbered acres, getting the tree was really easy. We'd just take a short walk down the hill, find a tree, cut it down, and carry it back home. Then, as we

Here I'm putting the glaze on a batch of Mini Orange Bundt Cakes, which I love to make for gifts and parties.

MINI ORANGE BUNDT CAKES
RECIPE IS ON PAGE 113.

Decorating for the holidays is much more fun when shared with a friend—
Teri and I laugh often at this time of year.

were serenaded by Elvis Christmas tunes with my mom singing backup, my dad would fashion a handmade wooden tree stand, and the tree would be placed on top of a huge cabinet in the living room.

The magic always began when my mom unpacked my Grandma Cecelia's old glass ornament collection. As each ornament was carefully unwrapped, I'd be overwhelmed with emotion, because these were ornaments from a special Grandma I never had the chance to meet. After all the ornaments were carefully placed on the tree, we'd hang the tinsel and then stand back to watch our dad climb the ladder and place Grandma's star at the top of the tree. It was then officially Christmas.

Once Christmas began, it was a baking and crafting extravaganza for me. Jam thumbprints, snowballs, and sugar cookies with

Colin's Tree Farm

$\mathcal{E}$very year, Colin and I like to throw a big holiday party for our friends. When we moved into our home on Peone Prairie, one of Colin's dreams for our property was to start a Christmas-tree farm, just for friends and family. His thought was that each year, when everyone came for the party, they could get their trees at the same time.

Colin spent months researching which trees would work best for our growing conditions and planning everything out. The area where the trees were to be planted was readied and irrigated. So, on a perfect autumn day, 300 trees were planted and Colin's dream was set in motion. Every day when he came home from work, he'd happily gaze out the window and over the garden to his tree farm. December came, and the tiny trees were covered in pristine snow.

In spring the snow began to melt away, and the trees began to show a tiny bit of growth. But, as spring turned to summer and the temperature began to rise, we noticed a small family of ground squirrels appearing and the trees slowly vanishing. As they feasted on the trees' tender roots, the family multiplied and established a little city. Soon all the trees disappeared, and Colin became Elmer Fudd.

Although all the trees were lost, the tree farm is not gone forever. Colin is still hard at work, carefully planning a takeover of Ground Squirrel City and creation of the farm of his dreams.

Celeste, in the middle here, and Teri enjoy Christmas as much as I do. And so does Celeste's dog Fagen.

crushed-candy windows were my favorites; and strung popcorn, construction-paper chains, and crayon shaving–waxed paper decorations were my specialties. My mom would bake batches upon batches of cardamom bread wreaths (her specialty) and make tarragon vinegar in beautiful old jars for gifts. My Grandpa Elliott would send an almond tower every year with smoked, roasted and salted, and blanched varieties, and I'd feel very fancy with such a sophisticated treat.

On Christmas Eve, just before bed, we were each allowed to open one gift, which was usually something like a great book or thrift-shop flannel jammies. We'd read *The Night Before Christmas* by the light of a kerosene lantern and then scamper up to the loft for an anticipation-filled night's sleep.

We'd all awaken at the break of dawn and make our way downstairs to find our stockings filled with goodies like oranges, cans of olives, and sardines. The rest of the day would be spent with my brother and sister, playing board games, sledding, building igloos, and having snowball fights. The season didn't end on that day, as our mom loved the holidays and kept the Christmas decorations up until Valentine's Day, when she replaced them with hearts.

CINNAMON BEAR

When I was a child, we lived a long way from friends' homes. So after several hours of visiting a family and munching on a potluck buffet, my mom and dad would gather us up and we'd start for home at about 7 p.m., which was perfect timing for us to catch *The Cinnamon Bear* as we sat through the long drive.

The Cinnamon Bear was an old-time radio show from the Thirties that was broadcast on the local radio station beginning on the first of December, and running each night up to Christmas Day. Since we never owned a television, the adventures of Paddy O'Cinnamon (the Cinnamon Bear) were a really big deal for my siblings and me. On the nights that we were at home, we'd all

The white winter landscape always gets me into the holiday spirit.

gather on my parents' bed and settle in for the broadcast. We never missed it.

Although *The Cinnamon Bear* is no longer on the radio, I was able to find the original episodes on CD, and listening to it is a tradition that Colin and I have carried on with our four boys. Every night, just before bedtime, we turn the lights down low and gather in the living room with lots of cozy blankets to listen to an episode. The adventures of Paddy O'Cinnamon remain one of the highlights of the season for us.

THE THOMPSON FAMILY CHRISTMAS

Now Colin and I have our own family, and Christmas is still the most wonderful time of the year. Christmas Eve

Be Careful What You Wish for

When I was a little girl, my mom ran a store out of a building on our property. A free store. The idea was that you could donate any items you no longer wanted, and you could also shop for things you might want or need. It was a great idea, and was pretty popular in our area, as few families had a lot of money.

One fall, one of my friends had just gotten a new outfit from a fancy "regular" store in town: purple corduroy pants with fancy back pockets and a matching corduroy vest. I loved it and wished so much that I had one too. I told my mom about my wish and she gave me the standard reply she gave to all of my wishes: "Be careful what you wish for, you just might get it." This didn't mean that I'd be getting one soon; it meant that, if it were meant to be, it would happen. And, in my mind, it meant it wasn't going to happen.

A few weeks later, another girl at school got the same outfit, which made me love it even more. As fall turned to winter and Christmastime rolled around, I had lost all hope. Then two days before Christmas, a big box arrived in the mail from an old family friend who wanted to donate to the free store some items that her daughter had recently outgrown. As I opened the box, I couldn't believe my eyes: There was my perfect little corduroy outfit, in green, and in my exact size. "You see?" my mom said. "Be careful what you wish for, you just might get it!"

There's much to do—making lists helps me plan and keeps me on track.

starts for us in the late afternoon, when we celebrate Mass at our church. The building is always stuffed with more people than usual, as families congregate to celebrate the season together. It's a really special time for Colin, when he visits with childhood friends who have come home for the holidays, and we're able to catch up with what's been going on in everyone's life. Excitement is in the air as the ushers pass out candy canes and listen to the children's wishes for Christmas.

We return home, just in time for dinner, and we all enjoy an appetizer extravaganza, followed by latte punch and an array of baked goods. Then games like "apples to apples" are played in jammies, and we all settle in to hear the final episode of *The Cinnamon Bear*. After another happy ending, our boys sit down to write letters to Santa, peppered with questions about the elves, whom they are definitely the most fascinated by.

After carefully selecting the perfect plate of goodies for Santa, and placing carrots and water on the porch for the reindeer, the boys check the window one last time, in hopes they'll see Rudolph's red glow. And then it's off to bed, where they're sure to dream of the day ahead.

Christmas morning starts bright and early for us, usually at about 6 a.m. After our younger children, Micah, Lucas, and Bongo, are all awake, they wake up their big brother, Cody, and together they pitter-pat their way upstairs to wake up Colin and me. Then it's out to the living room to open stockings and presents. Although the excitement is at an all-time high, the boys all very sweetly take turns opening gifts and admiring each other's surprises.

Gifts are followed by warm cinnamon rolls and hours upon hours of playing and sharing. Later on, in the afternoon, we all bundle up and head out for Grandma and Grandpa's, where the entire Thompson clan gathers for the rest of the day and evening. A big delicious meal with dishes brought by each family is shared, games are played, and fun is had by one and all.

Colin and I love continuing the traditions from our childhoods, and we have created new ones of our own. I look forward to sharing many of them with you here.

Serena

A Visit to the Tree Farm

Farmer Stan Clouse, who runs the ranch, is the perfect host.

My family feels lucky to live close to the Camden Tree Ranch, which is such a beautiful Christmas-tree nursery. It's a short drive from our home, through the sleepy little town of Elk into the woods of northern Spokane County. For several years the Edwards—Teri, Steve, and their daughters—have joined us for a tree hunt at this family-owned ranch, and we're back again this year to find that perfect Christmas tree. The snow is deep and it's cold, but we know there's hot cider waiting for us by the wood stove in the barn, where we'll warm ourselves and catch up on family news. Our tree hunt is a great way for us to start the holiday season and even better when shared with friends!

The day always begins with a fun ride in the tractor-pulled hay wagon to the upper field and the trees.

There's a lot of laughter . . .

. . . and usually a few snowballs
thrown before we begin the all-
important search for our trees.

Camden
Ranch
CHRISTMAS
TREES

Teri and her son-in-law, Emil, smile as the Edwards family votes on this tree.

The Thompson family treks around and around the ranch, searching for just the right tree.

With everyone in agreement, Steve cuts the tree.

This could be the one but . . .

. . . after much searching, my son Cody proclaims
another to be just right.

Ways to Ward Off the Chill

Whenever we go on an outdoor winter excursion, we take along a few munchies and thermoses filled with warm drinks that appeal to everyone in the family. No matter how cold our fingers and toes become, we know they'll quickly warm up once we're sipping hot chocolate, coffee, or cider. Here are some things we especially enjoy.

SPICED CIDER

Pour a quart of apple cider into a heavy saucepan. Add ¼ cup brown sugar, several whole cinnamon sticks (break them in half), a few cardamom pods, and a generous teaspoon of whole cloves, and simmer over low heat until the spices flavor the cider—about 25 minutes. Strain into a thermos.

WARM LEMONADE

Heat a quart of homemade or purchased lemonade over medium heat until warm—pink lemonade will be extra festive. (If you make your own, sweeten it with honey instead of sugar.) Pour into a thermos. Take some small peppermint sticks along and when you serve the hot lemonade, put one in each cup as a flavorful stirrer.

SPICED HOT CHOCOLATE

Make hot chocolate from the recipe on a container of cocoa powder (Dutch-processed cocoa has the richest flavor). Season it with ground cinnamon, nutmeg, and cloves, and stir in a little vanilla extract. Experiment to find the amount of seasoning you like. For extra richness, stir in chopped bittersweet chocolate until melted—add 1 tablespoon per cup of cocoa. Pour into a thermos. Take mini marshmallows or a can of aerosol whipped cream along to top each serving.

HOT MOCHA

Mix equal parts of brewed coffee and homemade cocoa (follow the recipe on the cocoa-powder container). Add sugar to make the mocha sweet or bittersweet as you prefer. Pour into a thermos. For a special treat, take along some chilled whipped cream in a small thermos, and put a dollop on each cup when you serve the mocha. Shake ground cinnamon, cocoa powder, or chocolate shavings on top.

CHAI LATTE

Steep chai tea bags in hot milk. Remove the tea bags and pour the milk mixture into a thermos for delicious chai tea lattes to ward off the cold!

WARM MUNCHIES

Prepare Sweet and Salty Nuts (page 112) or Dark Chocolate Mint Cookies (page 120). While fresh and warm from the oven, wrap first in foil, then in a kitchen towel, and pack in a tiny cooler to keep warm. Or simply wrap in foil and later quickly warm atop a woodstove at your tree farm.

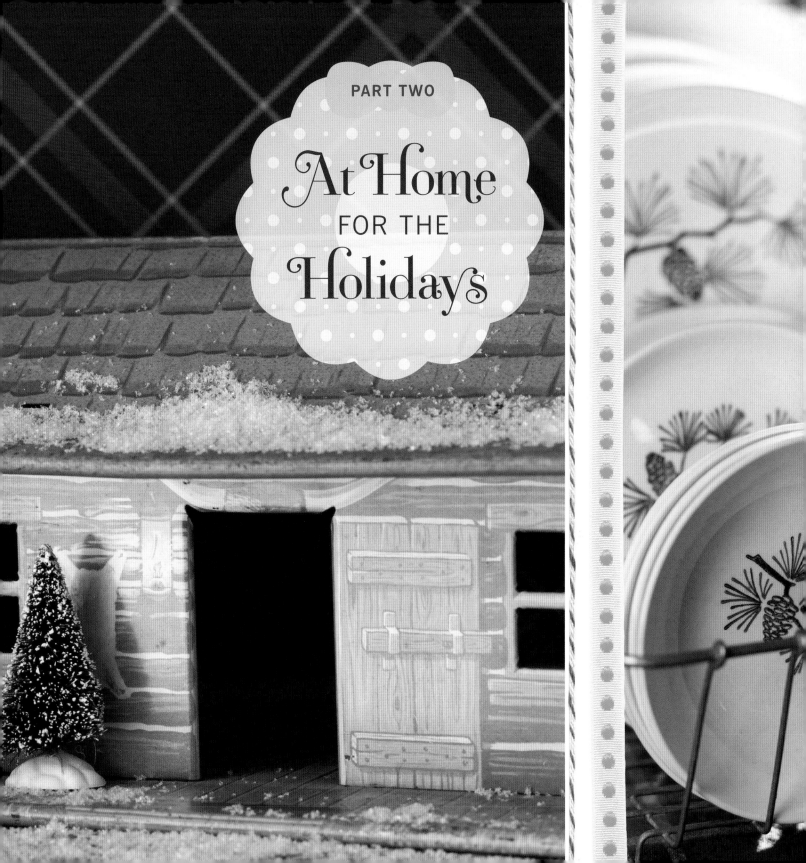

PART TWO

At Home
FOR THE
Holidays

Holiday Welcome

My front porch is an extension of my indoor Christmas decorating. It gives me an opportunity to decorate another room, and offers a great way to set the holiday tone before guests even enter my home. May everyone who visits see my love of Christmas and feel especially welcome!

I mixed handmade and vintage red-and-white-print pillows collected from estate sales to add Christmas cheer to the white painted chairs on my front porch.

My front porch glows with a tree (my second), and evergreen garlands drape the windows and door. The fabric bunting that hangs from the ceiling creates such a cheerful welcome—I had a good time making it, too (see directions at right to make one yourself).

HOLIDAY SCALLOPED BUNTING

The bunting is made from assorted fabrics cut into small panels, each two-scallops-wide and layered three-deep; these are placed side-by-side and sewn together. Here's how:

Make the pattern: Choose a bowl the size you'd like the scallops to be. Use it as a pattern, drawing around it twice to make a double scallop and then drawing straight up on each side to make a panel like the ones in the photo. Make this panel the length you want for the bottom layer of your bunting. Add ½-inch seam allowance on each straight edge. Copy this pattern twice, making each copy an inch or so shorter than the previous one.

Cut the panels: From assorted colorful fabrics, cut enough of the longest pattern to span the opening where you plan to hang it. (Don't include the seam allowance when figuring out how many panels you need.) Cut the same number of medium-length panels, and the same number of short panels.

Assemble the bunting: With all the fabric right-side-up and using pieces cut from three different fabrics for each, layer the panels with the longest piece on the bottom and the shortest on the top. Pin at the top of each. Arrange the panels side-by-side in a random sequence—so the adjacent fabrics are different. Then, with the right sides together, sew the panels together to make one long strip. Press the seam allowances open. Staple or tack the bunting where you want to display it,

I've come to visit my friend Teri and admire her holiday decorations.

Merry Christmas

A vintage kitchen canister with a classic red-and-white-plaid finish has become the perfect container for greenery. Propped next to the door are red children's skis, a favorite find from an old farm where we traded goods.

Teri's front porch cupboard (from an old post office) is filled with some of her favorite campy finds. The green and cream shelves set off the red plaids, miniatures, and fun signs.

Trimmed with green and set in the snow at this time of year, Teri's garden shed is the perfect canvas for her campy Christmas style.

An aged lake sign, found at an old fishing camp, adds perfect local color in the background at Teri's garden shed.

An old mailbox makes a great place to display a little greenery.

Make Every Corner Bright
• greetings •

Don't miss any opportunity to greet family and friends during the holidays. A "Merry Christmas" on the chalkboard or a "Happy Holidays" on the front porch is the perfect way to welcome your guests.

COUNTERCLOCKWISE FROM TOP LEFT Chalkboards are ideal for delivering favorite holiday greetings. You can easily personalize the message if you like. ❊ On my front porch, a vintage type-writer displays a welcoming message. ❊ Scrabble games have several copies of every letter—enough to spell out a neat little Christmas greeting for anyone you know.

A simple basket of bright glass ornaments gets into the holiday spirit when dusted with snow.

At my friend Celeste's, old seasonal lawn decorations are a joyful sight in the deep snow.

Originally a lawn ornament, this small deer figure has been transplanted to the porch, where he adds a woodland touch to the Christmas décor.

On a visit to Celeste's house one day just before Christmas, I was so touched to see the Farm Chicks sign she and her husband, Dan, had made as a special welcome. She's on my left here, and Teri is on my right.

Artificial trees and a giant Santa portrait make Celeste's front porch warm and homey despite the chill in the air.

Even Santa needs a place to hang his lunch box.

Nancy & Sally

If our lives had a theme, Nancy's and Sally's would be "Life is a Party!" Sally and Nancy are longtime friends and business partners who I met when they became vendors at The Farm Chicks Antiques Show, an annual event I started with my friend Teri, who has since retired. They call themselves the Happy Campers and, appropriately, both own travel trailers they've decorated and turned into darling little living areas in their backyards. (You can see that Teri and I enjoyed joining the fun in this photo of Nancy's trailer.)

Since both Nancy and Sally are avid collectors, these extra living spaces are good excuses for more collections and holiday decorations. At Christmastime—which officially begins right after Thanksgiving—lighted trees, wreaths, and twinkling lights are brought out, and the decorating extravaganza begins. After the outdoors is thoroughly trimmed, more decorating starts inside, interspersed with the occasional Bunco party, impromptu get-togethers, and good times.

On Christmas Eve, all the fun culminates in one big party at Nancy's, where a steady stream of visitors comes to visit, feast on tamales, and make merry. Each year a custom holiday song is created, either by a neighbor or Nancy and her boys, and then performed with much craziness and animation.

Later that night, when Sally is back at home, she's sure to bake up a batch of her mom's pfefferneuse, which for years didn't taste quite right. After lots of tinkering, Sally realized Mom had accidentally given out an incomplete recipe. Luckily, the recipe is now whole, and the cookies are perfect and will be served at the final Christmas celebration of the year. But for Nancy and Sally, a New Year will be dawning, and the parties will never really end.

The Decorated Tree

My holidays officially begin with the decorating of the Christmas tree (or trees), and this is a task my family looks forward to for weeks. As we all gather around to hang lights and ornaments on the green branches, we are thankful for this special time together.

Here is Teri's family Christmas tree all decorated for the holidays—this year she's chosen to use lots of white, accented with the red stripes of little candy canes. Those snowballs are yarn pompoms, which are fun and easy to make (see opposite).

MAKE IT

SNOWBALL POMPOM ORNAMENTS

Wrap yarn around three fingers approximately 80 times. Carefully remove. Tie a 5-inch piece of yarn around the center of the loops and secure tightly with a double knot. Cut all the loops open with scissors. Fluff the pompom and trim to form a perfect little snowball. Using a needle, insert clear button thread into the middle of the snowball; pull through and tie off with a double knot to create a hanging loop.

TIP

For easier cleanup of tiny yarn scraps, work over newspaper when trimming the pompoms.

This old galvanized tub makes a cute and tidy disguise for Teri's tree stand.

Make Every Corner Bright
• bulbs & balls •

Christmas decorations are beautiful on trees, but I love them even more displayed all around my home. They transform everyday objects into fun holiday displays and make everything feel cheery and bright.

COUNTERCLOCKWISE FROM TOP LEFT Family ornaments passed down through generations bring forth happy memories when arranged in a shallow bowl with some sprigs of greenery. ❋ Holiday light bulbs are so colorful, and Celeste loves to display them in groups. They're sweet to look at—especially in a covered candy jar frosted with snow. ❋ Mini ornaments are great Christmas collectibles. Little glass balls like these are fun to display in their original boxes if you have them. ❋ Filled with teeny glass balls, this vintage Serv-I-Car makes a fun holiday centerpiece or can be set on a mantel or anywhere you'd like a bit of whimsy. ❋ An old toolbox makes a great display piece for small holiday collectibles. Celeste created a rainbow of bulbs in this one.

My friend Nancy tucks huge, vintage industrial light bulbs into the branches of her Christmas tree. They're a quirky addition to her beautiful tree with its solid-color gold, silver, and copper balls, its ribbons and stars.

HOLIDAY SPRITZ COOKIE RECIPE IS ON PAGE 116.

MAKE IT

SILHOUETTE ORNAMENTS

Capture the likeness of loved ones with these sweet little ornaments—they're fun to tie onto gifts. Cover small wooden craft plaques with pretty paper and drill a hole at the top-center. Take digital profile snapshots and size them to fit your paper-covered wooden plaque; then print on the wrong side of the paper you'll be using for the silhouettes. Cut out the silhouettes and glue them, photo side down, onto the plaques. Add a thread or string hanging loop.

What could be cuter for a tree-decorating party than tree-shaped Holiday Spritz cookies served on a green plate with milk in a vintage holly-patterned glass?

My friend Celeste's Christmas tree glows with more than 2,000 vintage ornaments. They're all glass, in many colors and sizes. It's magical. The big burlap sacks you see nearby hold wrapped gifts for each person in her family.

Celeste labels each gift sack with a simple tag bearing the recipient's name. The plain fabric keeps the focus on the tree until Christmas morning. Then, when the bags are opened, everyone's brightly wrapped gifts come tumbling out.

Danny

Joe's Tinfoil Star

Teri was my business partner in the Farm Chicks for nearly seven years until she retired. Her parents, like mine, are good at finding magic in humble things during the holidays. I love this story about a Christmas early in her marriage.

Teri and Steve lived in a remote, small, eastern Montana town. Teri's in-laws, Joe and Sandy, were coming to spend Christmas with them, and she wanted everything to be nice. She baked cookies, made candy, cleaned the house, and planned the meals for their visit. She decorated with what she had, but since this was just their second Christmas together, she didn't have a lot. The closest shopping was nearly a three-hour drive away and, with a baby, she didn't go that often. So she made do with what she had.

Teri and Steve decided to wait until Joe and Sandy arrived to decorate the tree. After dinner that first evening she brought out a jar of spritz cookies and cups of hot cocoa, and Steve plugged in a Bing Crosby Christmas tape. They strung lights, hung ornaments, and draped silver tinsel on every branch. When they were finished, Joe asked what they put on the top. Teri told him she didn't have anything and went about cleaning up. About 15 minutes later he handed her a shiny, silver top ornament. He had cut a piece of cardboard into the shape of a star and covered it with tinfoil. That was so typical him! He's from that era where people knew how to make do: If you didn't have something, you improvised.

Teri says that throughout the years she's used other tree toppers, but nothing feels quite as right as that perfectly imperfect, shiny tinfoil star made 23 years ago. She still has it, and this year, she'll serve spritz cookies with hot cocoa and Steve will play the Bing Crosby Christmas CD while they decorate the tree and top it with Joe's star.

The Thompson family Christmas tree, enthusiastically decorated by our boys with yarn, candy canes, and colorful strung candies.

MAKE IT

STRUNG CANDY ORNAMENTS

To deck the tree or other greens with candies, look for types that can be easily strung, like these gummy wreaths. Some types of fancy ribbon candies also work. Thread a length of pretty ribbon through each candy and tie to make a loop.

The Gift of Giving
• gift wraps •

Sometimes the way a gift is wrapped can mean as much as what's inside. Use special containers that the recipient can keep, and attach tags and tie-ons to double the sentiment and the seasonal joy!

FROM LEFT TO RIGHT Presenting specially wrapped packages to friends is part of the fun! Here glass ornaments are delivered in an old metal feed scoop. ❋ Wrapping is quick and easy when the supplies are all organized in a common location. Besides, a drawer-full like this is inspiring! ❋ This homemade tote found at a thrift store is a great holder for tiny gifts.

A stack of colorfully wrapped gifts is a happy sight—even plain papers look festive when the assortment is pretty.

Take advantage of the many bold, colorful packaging materials that are available at holiday shops. Then embellish them with creative tie-ons like vintage corsages, candy, tiny ornaments, and ribbon.

TIP
Use pinking shears or scissors with another decorative edge to cut the felt.

GIFT CARD HOLDERS

A felt envelope makes opening the gift card as much fun as unwrapping the gift. To fashion an envelope, cut a strip of felt about ½-inch wider than the card and twice as long plus 1 inch. Place the card approximately in the middle of the strip. Fold up the bottom end of the strip and fold down the top end, adjusting the card so the top of the strip overlaps the bottom; crease the folds with your fingers. Unfold the top, remove the card, and hot-glue the bottom pocket together along the left and right side edges. Cut a vertical slit opening in the top flap for a buttonhole; affix a pretty, fabric-covered button to the pocket, opposite the slit.

Things like a vintage picnic tin, thermos, and ice-cream box are creative containers that can be used to hold gifts. Whimsical items such as tiny toy cars, vintage hotel keys, and cupcake toppers add a special touch as tie-ons.

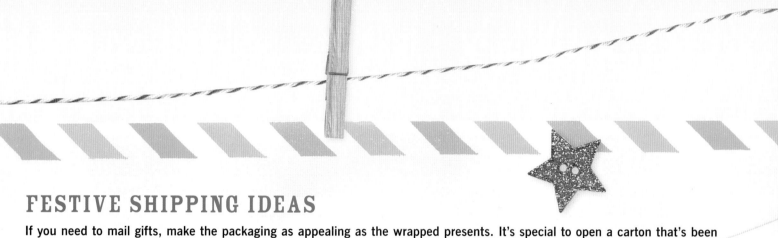

FESTIVE SHIPPING IDEAS

If you need to mail gifts, make the packaging as appealing as the wrapped presents. It's special to open a carton that's been well thought-out, with unique touches that show the recipient your love. Try color-coordinated looks or cushion the boxes with something that gives a clue to their contents.

FROM LEFT TO RIGHT White paper candy-striped with red accents looks fresh and crisp nestled in peppermints. The big package is a cookbook, and an old, small book serves as a gift tag. ❋ Fragrant greens make a festive travel nest for wrapped packages and can be used by the recipient for decorating her home. ❋ Flea markets are a great source of inexpensive printed material like vintage sheet music. Crumple up some to cushion gifts for a friend who loves music.

Wreaths & Garlands

It's amazing what a difference wreaths and garlands can make in turning your everyday home into a holiday home. Whether they are simple, fresh greenery or specially crafted creations, they are always a perfect holiday adornment.

This welcome sign is a favorite find of mine from The Farm Chicks Antiques Show. I topped it with a rope of fresh greens to welcome visitors to my holiday home.

MAKE IT

PAPER GARLAND

This delicate paper garland adds a sweet accent to greens, or even to a tree. Use a circular paper punch to cut out circles from pretty patterned scrapbook paper. With their right sides out, glue the circles in pairs over a long piece of baker's twine, spacing several inches apart.

To make her family room all ready for guests, Teri strung fresh green garlands across the bright red walls; they frame an old holiday sign and a fun white cupboard with its display of festive goodies.

Make Every Corner Bright
• natural accents •

My home doesn't feel fully Christmas-y until I've added in some greenery and pinecones. When I lived in Alaska, surrounded by nothing but tundra, my parents would send me a big box of evergreen clippings from home. It made all the difference. Not only did my apartment smell like cedar and pine, it felt homey—like Christmas the way I always knew it to be.

COUNTERCLOCKWISE FROM TOP LEFT Clippings from the backyard are a quick-and-easy way to dress up a table. I placed these in bright-green flower buckets and arranged them along a striped table runner. ❄ Fresh red and cream roses massed in a big container make a gorgeous center-piece; Celeste arranged these in a concrete garden tub, where they look especially pretty under the bell lampshades with the pine wreaths as a backdrop. ❄ Pine tree branches are a long-lasting decoration—you don't need to put them in water. Set in a vintage enamel cup, these shelter a wee Santa on Teri's front porch. ❄ Old Spokane Crescent Christmas shopping bags, found at a yard sale, make the perfect cheery red container for pine boughs.

Teri's mantel looks so festive adorned with lots of greens, large pine cones, and a vintage garland of paper bells that spells out Merry Christmas.

Groupings of wreaths add a homey touch to any room. Celeste has added a simply decorated fresh wreath to each window in this bay and topped them with a lush swag of greens.

MAKE IT

HOLIDAY YARN-BALL WREATH

This wreath is fun to make with friends or your kids; use whatever colors of yarn you like: Wrap a 12-inch round Styrofoam wreath form with yarn or fabric strips until completely covered. Make a hanger from the same fabric or two lengths of yarn, cutting and tying around the top of the wreath. Wrap twelve 4-inch and twelve 3-inch Styrofoam balls with yarn in a random pattern until completely covered; tuck the end of the yarn under the wraps. Then, using a hot-glue gun, randomly glue the 4-inch balls onto the wreath. Allow to dry until firm. Randomly glue the 3-inch balls onto the wreath, filling in any gaps.

Christmas for Celeste

Walking into my friend Celeste's house during the holidays is a warming experience. Christmas surrounds you and gives you a great big hug. When she recalls her Christmases of long ago while being raised by her grandparents on a farm in rural Montana, two things shine brightly in her memory: Santa always came and Christ was always born.

Celeste relates that, as the sun went down on Christmas Eve, Grandpa would hoist himself onto the roof of their farmhouse and spread oats all about as Celeste, her sisters, and Grandma watched. Santa's reindeer would need this sustenance to continue their flight through the night. Grandma would point out the North Star, and then they'd make their way inside to get the girls scrubbed up before bed.

The Christmas Eve bath was an event Celeste looked forward to with much excitement. Grandpa would carry water from the well inside for Grandma to boil and pour into a big galvanized feed tub. Grandma would add a few drops of Avon perfume, and then she'd pull out her accordion.

Celeste and her sisters would march around the tub to the music until Grandpa declared, "I see loaves!" (baby bottoms), and plop them into the scented bath.

Later, once warm and snug in her attic bed, Celeste could hear her grandmother call out, "Daddy! We better listen for the weather!" She'd listen through the floorboards to the National Weather Service radio announcer give a very important update: "Wait a minute! Wait a minute! Santa has just passed through North Dakota and is on his way to Montana!" All was perfect in their happy home. At first light on Christmas morning, Grandpa would hoist himself back onto the roof, where he'd declare that all the oats had been eaten and that the roof was covered in reindeer tracks. "You girls did a good thing, saving the reindeer," he'd say.

It's no surprise that Christmas is still Celeste's favorite time of the year. Just as her grandmother filled burlap feed sacks with homemade gifts, Celeste now does the same. Hers is a truly happy home.

A wreath of fresh greens looks inviting on Celeste's front door, inside the decorative screen.

This pinecone wreath, purchased 25 years ago on Teri's honeymoon, is just as beautiful today as it was then, and looks great displayed on an old, weathered sled.

HOLIDAY SPICE LOGS RECIPE IS ON PAGE 122.
CHOCOLATE-DRIZZLED ALMOND MACAROONS RECIPE
IS ON PAGE 121.

Cupboards & Corners

At holiday time, I love to bring a cheerful Christmas spirit into all the corners and cupboards of my home. Sometimes it's just simple touches and groupings of like items that make everything look special and festive.

This sweet little green chair adds a fun surface to the dessert bar for a party at Teri's. The vintage enamelware and tiny, child-size glasses with crocheted cozies make the perfect containers to hold colorful candies. In the glass jar to its left are Teri's Holiday Spice Logs, and in the log dish below them are Chocolate-Drizzled Almond Macaroons.

A display of baking supplies is a simple, yet darling way to liven up a kitchen cupboard. Glass jars keep the shelves tidy and colorful.

Celeste used vintage sign letters to spell out a holiday message on an old hanging shelf—this is easy to do, and heartfelt.

Filled with a collection of vintage toys and surrounded by the colors of Christmas, this old country cupboard is part of an inviting entryway at Celeste's.

VINTAGE-FUNNEL TREES

My friend Chris fashions great "trees" by inverting and stacking old metal funnels. To make, start with a small branch and slide the funnels onto it, one after another, until the tree is the desired height. Use another funnel for a base, inserting the branch into it, or insert the branch into a small gravel-filled plant pot and top with moss. Adorn with ornaments if desired.

Make Every Corner Bright
• holiday houses •

Miniature houses are a favorite collectible of mine and, like all true collectors, I will never have enough. Now I find myself looking for new places to tuck them during the holidays. I love how these miniature objects can make me so happy.

CLOCKWISE FROM TOP RIGHT This grouping of vintage cardboard Putz houses, each complete with its own evergreen tree, makes a colorful display arranged in a wine rack. ❄ This old Marx toy cabin becomes part of a miniature winter wonderland with the addition of tiny trees and a sprinkling of vintage mica snow. ❄ Why not make a tiny Putz house the star of the show? Mini cake stands like this provide the perfect platforms; look for them in home accessories stores. ❄ Adding ribbon and a wreath to a plain cardboard house makes it ready for the season. Don't forget to place a tree inside! ❄ Consider using Christmas jewelry as an adornment on crafts projects. Teri added a wreath of faux greens to this holiday pendant and then hung it between the windows on the mini house.

MAKE IT

WRAPPING-PAPER VILLAGE

Add a special touch to any holiday village by personalizing it with siding made of your favorite wrapping papers. Basic village kits are available at most craft stores. Use the kit pattern pieces as a guide for cutting the paper and then attach it with a glue stick.

A bucketful of Christmas wrap adds color to a corner, and is as cute as it is convenient.

Foil-wrapped candies and a few glass balls tucked by my friend Nancy into sprigs of fresh greens transform a grouping of old cowboy collectibles into a Christmas display.

A bright-blue kitchen chair sporting a darling wreath of kitschy collectibles perks up this fieldstone fireplace.

An open cupboard creatively arrayed with a random assortment of Christmas items creates a warm living room backdrop. Teri creatively covered the little village houses with wrapping paper (see page 69).

Christmas Collections

My mother-in-law, Mary Jane, has some great collections that take center stage in her home during the holidays. Her decorating begins when she creates a scenic Christmas village atop the piano in the family room. As she unpacks and carefully places each little house, each a gift from her children over the years, the scene begins to twinkle with cheer. All the grandchildren love sitting on the piano bench and gazing up at the magical scene.

Next comes the nativity set, which Mary Jane and my father-in-law, Pete, fondly remember collecting during their days as a newlywed couple on a tight budget. On a trip to Woolworth's department store back then, they spotted a huge display of bins containing nativity pieces—several styles of each. Fortunately, the store was really quiet, making it easy for them to take their time and choose carefully. A small crowd began to gather and soon completely surrounded them, admiring their choices and chiming in with opinions on which pieces were best. After much deliberation

and help from the onlookers, Mary Jane and Pete came away with a set they truly loved, and now we all do too.

I cherish the fact that both of these collections have meaning. Whether for sentimental memories or inherent charm, I think most people have a holiday collection they cherish. For my mother, it is the glass ornaments that first belonged to her mother. Another collection of Pete and Mary Jane's that I especially love is a group of personalized Santa mugs, in which they serve warm spiced cider while they decorate their tree. As you can see on page 77, where the mugs sit on the counter with my baked treats, I like to borrow them from time to time. For me, it's my collection of chalkware choirboys, a favorite find from a thrift shop. It's not perfect, but it's dear, and even though some of the choristers are chipped, they all make me smile. If you decide to start your own Christmas collection, be sure it makes you smile too—and let it recall a happy memory that makes it special.

Groupings of like colors create a harmonious scene with lots of impact. Here, the many shades of white glow on Nancy's mantel.

SNOWBALLS RECIPE, PAGE 116.

CHOCOLATE-COVERED PEANUT BUTTER BALLS RECIPE, PAGE 114.

BUTTER CUTOUTS RECIPE, PAGE 114.

This eye-catching display of desserts includes an oversized enamelware mug filled with Snowball cookies to give a playful illusion of marshmallows floating on a cup of hot cocoa, a glass bowl of pretty, Chocolate-Covered Peanut Butter Balls, and a tray of classic, tree-shaped Butter Cutouts.

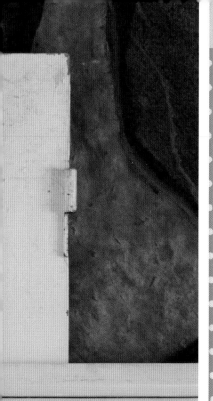

MAKE IT

COLORFUL CONE TREES

Handmade Christmas trees like these are so colorful—I love to group them in a cubby for a quirky display. They're a snap to create: Simply cover Styrofoam cones with pretty paper, yarns, greenery, or fabric strips, and hot-glue into place.

Kitchens & Pantries

It's natural that, with all the baking and special meal preparations, my kitchen becomes the gathering place for family and friends during the holidays. I would guess yours does too. Let's all pull out the Christmas dishes for display, jar up the colorful candy, and bring Christmas into our kitchens!

Show off your baked goods by displaying them on a variety of colorful cake stands. The green stand in front displays my Tiny Lemon Meringue Tarts, and behind it is my boys' favorite, Marble Bread.

TINY LEMON MERINGUE TARTS
RECIPE IS ON PAGE 124.

MARBLE BREAD
RECIPE IS ON
PAGE 112.

No need to frost these delicate little Butter Cutout cookies. Just dress up with a dusting of confectioners' sugar, drizzle with melted chocolate, or sandwich together with raspberry jam.

RASPBERRY THUMBPRINTS RECIPE IS ON PAGE 119.

BUTTER CUTOUTS RECIPE IS ON PAGE 114.

I've been baking my Raspberry Thumbprint cookies since I was a little girl. They're so cute on this pink, tiered vintage cake stand.

TOASTED-ALMOND BISCOTTI RECIPE IS ON PAGE 120.

MAKE IT

FRUIT BASKET GIFT WRAP

Green plastic fruit baskets are readily available in the produce section of most markets. They make the perfect container for sharing home-baked goodies during the holiday season. Line the basket with parchment paper and then simply weave a ribbon through the openings and tie off with a bow. Fill with a favorite sweet, like these Toasted-Almond Biscotti.

My kitchen is the gathering place of my home year round. Decked out with fresh greens and yummy homemade sweets, it's ready to welcome friends. The old Santa painting above the window is a favorite find from the *Country Living* Fair.

Make Every Corner Bright
• kitchen treasures •

When I'm at home, the kitchen is my favorite place to be, so it makes sense that I have lots of kitchen collectibles. Dishes, cookie cutters, even syrup dispensers can become Christmas decorations.

COUNTERCLOCKWISE FROM TOP LEFT A collection of old Pyrex Christmas-holly mugs on a small rack makes a cute kitchen display. And cake stands, when they're not needed for desserts, are good for showing off mini trees or other holiday bits. ❄ This collection of vintage pine-cone dinnerware belongs to Teri. During the holidays, when she's not using them, she keeps them on display in an old wire dish drainer. ❄ Potential display possibilities are never ending. These red- and green-capped syrup dispensers filled with baubles create a funky and decorative grouping. ❄ I love old Christmas cookie cutters. When I'm not actually cutting dough with them, I like to show them off in a glass pantry jar.

These days, no one stores flour in a dispenser like this vintage metal wall box. But, for the holidays, it's proud to hold old ornaments.

MAKE IT

"MERRY" BANNER

Set off your display with a small message banner made of patterned scrapbooking papers. Cut triangles from assorted red papers. Use a stencil to outline the needed letters on green papers. Cut them out (use a craft knife to cut interior details). Affix a letter to each triangle with a glue stick. Arrange the triangles to spell your message and then hot-glue a length of ribbon along the top.

An array of footed jars filled with holiday candy can instantly brighten up open shelves or countertops and make the whole kitchen feel like a happier place to be.

MAKE IT

HOLIDAY SHELF LINER

Cover open shelves with your favorite wrapping paper to create a festive feel throughout the kitchen—wrap the paper over the edge for full effect. For a wipe-able surface, you can cover the paper with clear Con-Tact paper.

PAPER-LINED CUPBOARDS

Cupboards are easily livened up for the holidays: Simply line the backs and glass doors with colorful wrapping paper affixed with a little double-stick tape.

A Special Artist: Chris

I first met my friend Chris when she and her sisters were holding a yard sale. I was drawn to their sisterly banter and history of growing up together on their family farm. And, as our friendship has grown, I've loved listening to her stories about their creative and loving parents, Jeanne and Fritz. They are stories of what I imagine is the perfect childhood.

Fritz and Jeanne grew up in the Great Depression and learned to make do with what they had—a trait they passed on to Chris and her siblings. One Fourth of July, the kids complained, "there's nothing to do!" So Jeanne suggested a parade, and four of the kids marched through the three-block town. The next year, cousins joined in, and now every year the Fourth of July parade draws thousands of visitors to their sleepy little hometown.

Chris has often told me the focus was definitely not on material gifts at Christmastime in her childhood; rather, it was on the gift of family and time with one another. Other gifts were handmade, like the doll clothes Jeanne would carefully stitch for the girls or special Christmas treats baked for neighbors. Chris has always loved art and would practice her skills every chance she'd get. Her parents were full of compliments: "What a wonderful artist you are!" they'd say. One year when Chris returned home from college for the holidays, her mom had a surprise: a huge envelope filled with Chris' life's work—school assignments, art projects, and special recognitions. It's a gift Chris cherishes along with her happy memories.

Chris grew up to be an amazing artist and crafter. Several of her paintings adorn the walls of my home, and her Funnel Christmas Trees (see page 67 to make) now dwell in our friend Celeste's home. All of us who are lucky enough to own Chris's special creations are thankful to have a piece of her to appreciate on a daily basis.

Trimmed with greens, mini trees, and fun collectibles, Celeste's warm, inviting kitchen is ready for holiday guests.

A salvaged old window, framed in cedar boughs, is the focal point of her holiday kitchen. It fills the pass-through over the kitchen sink, so it's visible from the dining room beyond too.

Homemade Gifts

MINI MERINGUE STARS RECIPE IS ON PAGE 123.

Homemade gifts were the only gifts we could afford to give when I was a child. One of my favorites to create was soap snowballs. They were really easy to make. I'd take a bar of Ivory soap, grate it up with a cheese grater, add a few drops of water, and shape the flakes into little spheres that looked a lot like snowballs. After they sat for a day, I'd wrap them up (three to a pack); then they were ready to give out as gifts.

Homemade gifts are still my favorite type of gift to give, and I love baking and packaging an assortment of goodies for friends and for Colin's employees. I shop for colorful little boxes, tins, and bags that will be perfect for packaging the treats. The night before the treats are delivered, I get started baking right after dinner. Batch after batch are made, well into the night. And, when everything is baked, my favorite part is to wrap up everything as special as possible. After all, nothing shows you care more than a heartfelt homemade gift.

Celeste uses common objects such as this desktop organizer and old scale as great holiday display pieces.

The Gift of Giving
• food wraps •

Everyone appreciates a gift of home-baked treats. Take just a little extra time to make them even more special by packaging them thoughtfully in creative ways.

MINI ORANGE BUNDT CAKES RECIPE IS ON PAGE 113.

DARK CHOCOLATE MINT COOKIES RECIPE IS ON PAGE 120.

FROM LEFT TO RIGHT These Mini Orange Bundt Cakes make lovely gifts: Choose a bright gift box, line it with a coordinating napkin, pop in a pair of cakes, top with a bit of waxed paper, and seal. They're good to serve at a holiday party, too. ❊ Share the recipe for these Dark Chocolate Mint Cookies by packaging them in a parchment-paper-lined vintage file box and tuck the recipe inside the lid. Your friend will appreciate the samples as much as the recipe! ❊ I love to fill unused vintage food containers, like these cottage-cheese tubs, with treats. Here I first placed the cookies in clear cellophane bags, tying them simply with ribbon. Easy, and a perfect way to wrap a gift for a teacher or mail carrier. ❊ For a quick and easy party favor that makes a pretty display too, wrap candy sticks with gift-wrapping paper: Just twist the ends to seal.

FROM LEFT TO RIGHT Share your homemade treats in glass canning jars. The raised star that decorates the Mason-brand variety gives them a true holiday touch (look for them at thrift stores). Top them off by attaching Christmas-paper cupcake liners to the lid using double-stick tape. ❄ Stock the pantry with a variety of sprinkles for all your holiday baking. If you're having a cookie-decorating party, package the toppings in cute jars and send them to your friends with an invitation. ❄ Vintage dairy bottles are fun containers for colorful holiday candies or small cookies like these irresistible melt-in-your-mouth Mini Meringue Stars. To close the jars, cut round paper lids that tightly fit inside the lip or lid from scrapbook cardstock. Make sure to leave a tab for easy lifting.

MINI MERINGUE STARS RECIPE IS ON PAGE 123.

Happy Memories

I love bringing a bit of retro Christmas into my home. Decorating with vintage toys and colorful plaids brings back those sweet memories of childhood holidays. And simple touches, like hanging a miniature wreath around the neck of a toy cow or spelling out a Christmas phrase with vintage letters, add a charming and homey note.

Propped atop an old picnic "basket," a vintage Santa candy box becomes the perfect house for a tiny Christmas tree.

THE Santa Claus BOOK

by IRENE SMITH

A cheerful jumble of mostly red Christmas and non-Christmas items comes together for a darling display.

Nancy has cleverly displayed some old family ski photos in a themed vignette.

Here Celeste used small childhood toys to decorate a twiggy Christmas tree.

This vintage light-up Santa tree topper, a gift to Teri from her mom, brings a smile to both young and old. He's sweet standing next to his box when something else tops Teri's tree.

A supply of mittens is good to have handy on a windowsill or table near the door, in case an impromptu snowball fight breaks out.

Vintage Christmas stockings bring back childhood memories; Nancy's is made of felt, with cute felt appliqués.

It's the Thought That Counts

When Colin and I were first married, we had very little money. Stretching each paycheck was a chore, but I knew we could do it. Having been raised by parents with modest means, I learned how to make the most out of what we had, and I've always joked that I could make soup from stones. Although I've never had to make stone soup, we came close a few times.

Christmastime always seemed to be an especially strapped time of year. Although Colin and I didn't really have money for gifts, Colin always made sure that he had something to give me. For several years in a row, as he chose each one, he surely could not have imagined that his choice would become the source for many a good laugh in the Thompson family, at his expense. In his mind, these were practical gifts, and I was a practical girl.

Year One—One gallon of distilled water (just what Serena needs for all of the ironing she does, he thought).

Year Two—Firewood (perfect for keeping the family nice and warm, he figured).

Year Three—A gardening book, titled *The Able Gardener,* about how to garden as a paraplegic in a wheelchair. (All he saw was a gardening book, and he knew I loved to garden). It was on that third Christmas, when I opened my gift and discovered I'd soon be learning how to garden from a wheelchair, that our son Cody looked at me cheerily and said, "Well, it's the thought that counts, Mom!" He was right, but we still had a very good laugh—and still do every time the story is recounted.

Now Colin knows that I'm still a simple girl and that I love simple things like junky old toy trucks or vintage farm toys. They make darling decorations around our home. Although they're not expensive, they're the perfect gifts for me.

I love using unsweetened coconut shreds to simulate snow in holiday displays—
they're a "green" alternative to synthetic snow for these barnyard miniatures.

This child-sized thermos makes
a perfect little vase.

MAKE IT

GUMDROP WREATH

Candies can add whimsical color at Christmas. I made this bright green wreath by wrapping a Styrofoam form with fabric strips until completely covered, and then hot-gluing gumdrops all over the surface. I think it's the perfect backdrop for this toy dairy truck and mini foil tree.

Here's a festive use for old flash cards and random old letter cutouts—arranged to spell out greetings and words for the season.

HAZELNUT ACORNS
RECIPE IS ON PAGE 111.

The Gift of Giving
· entertaining ·

This special season is all about spending time with family and friends. From beautiful table place settings to simple party favors and sweets, there are many charming touches to create for your celebrations, and they all show your guests how much you care.

FROM LEFT TO RIGHT Whether used as a garnish on a cake or served as a sweet snack, your guests will love these tiny chocolate-tipped Hazelnut Acorn treats. ❅ White Hot Chocolate looks so festive in colorful mugs on a bright tray. For a little added flavor and flair, dip the rim of each mug in warmed honey and then in crushed peppermint. Everyone will love it!

SWEET AND SALTY NUTS
RECIPE IS ON PAGE 112.

WHITE HOT CHOCOLATE RECIPE
IS ON PAGE 111.

MAKE IT

PAPER SERVING CONES

Make a bunch of festive paper cones to serve these Sweet and Salty Nuts at a Christmas or New Year's party. For each, cut a piece of pretty paper 8½-inch by 5½-inch (half a letter-size sheet) and a piece of waxed paper the same size. Affix the waxed paper to the wrong side of the pretty paper with double-stick tape. Then hold by one corner and roll diagonally into a cone, securing the overlapping edge with more tape. Fold up about ¾ inch at the pointy tip and staple in place. Fill with nuts just before serving and arrange in small containers where your guests can help themselves.

FROM LEFT TO RIGHT Vintage toy trucks, no matter their condition, make a fun addition to a display of afternoon treats. ✳ Going for family drives to see homes lighted for the holidays is one of my family's favorite things to do. Caramel corn is packaged in individual treat bags, cups for cocoa are stacked with cocktail napkins to prevent rattling, and then it's all easily carried to the car in an old enamelware pan. Don't forget the Christmas music! ✳ Coffee Latte Punch is a rich and creamy treat my family enjoys every Christmas Eve. It's fun to serve in a funky vintage punch set.

COFFEE LATTE PUNCH
RECIPE IS ON PAGE 110.

FROM LEFT TO RIGHT It's fun to mix plain and fancy when you share sweets and coffee with friends by the fire. Celeste's twist on this is scones under a glass dome on a pretty cake stand and coffee in whimsical, numbered mugs on a silver tray. ❋ Nothing says "Christmas" like hot spiced cider served in holiday holly mugs. If you don't have a favorite recipe, there's a good one on page 24. ❋ Beautiful silver and crystal place settings glow under nearby tree lights. Here Nancy has topped hers with vintage numbers and set them on an antique crocheted lace cloth.

MAKE IT

FELT STEMWARE COASTERS

This is such a cute way to protect your table: For each coaster, cut two circles of felt 1¾-inch larger in diameter than the base of the glass. Cut a 1-inch circle out of the center of one piece (the top) and then cut two 1¼-inch-long slits on opposite sides of the center hole. Punch out little stars or dots all around the top piece. Stack the two pieces and attach them ½-inch inside the perimeter with a glue gun. Use pinking shears to create a decorative edge. Slip onto the glass before filling.

Holiday Recipes

I am pleased to share some favorite holiday recipes that I serve to my family or package as gifts for special friends. I hope you and your family enjoy them as much as I do. Merry Christmas!

DRINKS

coffee latte punch

MAKES about 14 cups (14 servings)
WORKING TIME 15 minutes
TOTAL TIME 45 minutes plus 4 hours to chill

I have enjoyed this recipe at Teri's holiday parties. She received it from a sister twenty years ago and has served it every Christmas since. Even if you're not a big fan of brewed coffee, you'll still love this rich drink with its subtle flavor and creamy topping. It's sure to become one of your family traditions too! SHOWN ABOVE RIGHT.

- ⅓ cup instant coffee powder
- ½ cup sugar
- ½ gallon 2% milk (8 cups)
- 1 cup half-and-half
- ½ gallon vanilla ice cream

Prepare the coffee mixture: Heat 1 cup water to boiling in a medium-size saucepan. Add the instant coffee and sugar, and stir until dissolved. Set aside until cool.

Pour the coffee mixture into a large container and stir in the milk. Cover and refrigerate overnight or at least 4 hours.

Make the punch: Thirty minutes before serving, pour the coffee mixture into a large punch bowl. Stir in the half-and-half. Using a scoop, add the ice cream to the punch bowl and let sit until most of the ice cream has melted—approximately 25 minutes. Gently whisk the ice cream into the coffee mixture until incorporated. Serve.

TIP *You can substitute 1 cup of hot, double-strength brewed coffee or espresso for the instant coffee and water if you like. Sometimes I don't fully whisk in the ice cream; instead I leave it floating to the surface as a yummy sweet topping for each serving.*

white hot chocolate

MAKES about 6 cups (6 servings)
WORKING TIME 12 minutes
TOTAL TIME 12 minutes

This lightly sweet warm drink is best made with 2% milk (or even whole milk) to give it real creaminess. You can use a bar of white chocolate instead of the chips; just grate or chop into small pieces for quicker melting. SHOWN ON PAGE 105.

> 1 cup half-and-half
> 1 cup white chocolate chips (6 ounces)
> 1 quart 2% milk (4 cups)
> 1 teaspoon vanilla extract

Heat the half-and-half over low heat in a medium-size saucepan until warm but not boiling. Add the chocolate chips and whisk until they are completely melted and incorporated. Whisk in the milk and vanilla, and cook, whisking often, until heated through but not bubbling. Serve warm.

hazelnut acorns

MAKES 2 heaping cups dipped nuts
WORKING TIME 45 minutes
TOTAL TIME 1 hour 15 minutes

These little "acorns" are delicious holiday treats to have sitting out in a bowl or to use as woodsy adornments on cakes. Although they're a bit time consuming to make, they're well worth the effort! SHOWN ON PAGE 104.

> 2 cups hazelnuts (8 ounces)
> 1 cup milk chocolate chips (6 ounces)
> ½ cup chocolate jimmies (sprinkles)

Roast the nuts: Heat the oven to 350°F. Place the nuts on baking sheet and roast for approximately 10 to 15 minutes, or until lightly toasted and skins are blistered. Wrap the nuts in a kitchen towel and rub gently to remove skins (don't worry about skins that do not come off) and let them cool.

Create the acorns: Place the chocolate chips in a small microwave-safe bowl and microwave on medium-high for 30 seconds (milk chocolate is sensitive to high heat); remove and stir. If not completely melted, repeat the microwaving. Place the jimmies in another small, shallow bowl. One at a time, hold the hazelnuts by the tip and dip the base first into the melted chocolate and then into the jimmies. Place the dipped nuts on waxed paper and let sit until the chocolate is cool and firm.

sweet and salty nuts

MAKES 3 cups nuts
WORKING TIME 10 minutes
TOTAL TIME 30 minutes

These nuts are salty, yet sweet, and very simple to whip up. They're the perfect treat to have on hand for holiday parties or snacks. SHOWN ABOVE.

1½ tablespoons butter
1½ tablespoons brown sugar
 2 teaspoons honey
½ teaspoon salt
 3 cups assorted nuts such as cashews,
     pecan halves, walnut halves, and whole
     blanched almonds

Coat the nuts: Heat the oven to 350°F. Line a large baking sheet with parchment paper or foil. Place the butter, brown sugar, honey, and salt in a medium-size, microwave-safe bowl. Microwave on medium for 1 minute, until the butter is melted. Stir the butter mixture to combine. Add the nuts and stir to coat.

Bake the nuts: Pour the nuts onto a baking sheet, spreading evenly, and bake until deep golden brown—approximately 20 minutes—stirring occasionally. Cool on the baking sheet on a wire rack. Store in an airtight container.

marble bread

MAKES one 9- by 5-inch loaf (12 to 16 servings)
WORKING TIME 15 minutes
TOTAL TIME 1 hour 5 minutes

My boys love this sweet loaf and would be perfectly happy if they could have a slice for a snack every day. It's the perfect balance of chocolate and vanilla and is more like cake than bread. SHOWN ON PAGE 77.

 2 squares semisweet chocolate (2 ounces), chopped
1¾ cups all-purpose flour
 2 teaspoons baking powder
¼ teaspoon salt
½ cup unsalted butter (1 stick), softened
 1 cup sugar
 2 large eggs
 1 teaspoon vanilla extract
¼ cup sour cream
⅓ cup boiling water

Melt the chocolate: Place the chocolate in a small microwave-safe bowl and microwave on high for 30 seconds; remove and stir. If not completely melted, repeat the microwaving. Stir until smooth. Set aside.

Make the batter: Heat the oven to 350°F. Butter a 9- by 5-inch loaf pan, then dust with flour, knocking out excess. In a small bowl, whisk together the flour, baking powder, and salt. Cream the butter in a medium-size bowl with an electric mixer on medium-low speed until smooth—2 to 3 minutes. Add the sugar, beating until fluffy. Add the eggs and vanilla, beating until well combined. Add the flour mixture and beat until combined. Beat in the sour cream and then, with the mixer on

low speed, beat in the boiling water until just combined. Transfer 1 cup of the batter to a glass measuring cup; stir in the chocolate, mixing completely.

Bake the bread: Add the vanilla and chocolate batters in alternating spoonfuls to the prepared pan. Pass a knife blade in a zigzag path through the batters to create a marbled effect. Bake until a toothpick inserted in the center of the loaf comes out clean—approximately 45 to 50 minutes. Cool the cake in the pan on a wire rack. Store in an airtight container.

mini orange bundt cakes

MAKES twenty-four 2½-inch cakes
WORKING TIME 20 minutes
TOTAL TIME 35 minutes plus cooling

Mini Bundt cakes are perfect for holiday gift-giving because not only are they delicious, they're really easy (and cute) to package, as you can see in the photo on page 90. These are moist, with just the right orangey flavor. SHOWN ON PAGES 14 AND 90.

  1¾ cups all-purpose flour
  2 teaspoons baking powder
  ½ cup unsalted butter (1 stick), softened
  1 cup sugar
  2 large eggs
  2 teaspoons finely grated orange zest
  1 teaspoon vanilla extract
  ⅓ cup sour cream
  ⅓ cup freshly squeezed orange juice
    Orange Glaze (recipe follows)

Make the batter: Heat the oven to 350°F. Butter two mini fluted Bundt cake pans (each holding twelve 2½-inch cakes); then dust with flour, knocking out excess. Whisk together the flour and baking powder in a small bowl. Cream the butter in a medium-size bowl with an electric mixer on medium-low speed until smooth—2 to 3 minutes. Add the sugar, beating until fluffy. Add the eggs, orange zest, and vanilla, beating until well combined. Add the flour mixture, beating until just combined. Add the sour cream and orange juice, beating until just combined.

Bake the cakes: Divide the batter evenly among the cups in the prepared pans. Bake until a toothpick inserted in the center of a cake comes out clean—about 15 minutes. Cool the cakes in the pans on wire racks. Loosen the cakes from the pan using the tip of a knife, then invert the rack over the pan and turn the cakes out onto a platter. Drizzle with Orange Glaze.

Orange Glaze
Mix 1 tablespoon melted butter and 1 teaspoon finely grated orange zest in a small bowl. Stir in 1 cup confectioners' sugar until well blended. Stir in freshly squeezed orange juice 1 teaspoon at a time until the glaze reaches a good drizzling consistency (5 teaspoons orange juice is our preferred amount).

TIP *If you don't have a mini Bundt pan, you can use 24 muffin cups (2 pans), lined with cupcake liners, instead.*

butter cutouts

MAKES about thirty 2½-inch cookies
WORKING TIME 45 minutes
TOTAL TIME 1 hour 30 minutes plus chilling

I love these cookies. They're delicate and buttery—a simple cookie made sophisticated. The first time I had these, they were baked by my friend Hannelore for everyone who attended her wedding to Colin's good friend Calvin. I was so glad she was willing to share the recipe! SHOWN AT RIGHT.

  2 cups all-purpose flour
¼ teaspoon salt
  1 cup unsalted butter (2 sticks), softened
½ cup sifted confectioners' sugar
  1 teaspoon vanilla extract
    Colored sugars or sprinkles, raspberry jam,
      or melted chocolate, for garnishes (optional)

Make the dough: Mix the flour and salt in a small bowl. Cream the butter in a large bowl with an electric mixer on medium speed until smooth—2 to 3 minutes. Add the confectioners' sugar and vanilla, beating until well combined. Lower the mixer speed to medium-low and gradually beat in the flour mixture. Transfer the dough to a piece of plastic wrap and pat into an 8-inch disk. Wrap with the plastic and refrigerate for 1 hour.

Cut the cookies: Divide the dough in half. Place one portion of the dough on a lightly floured surface and roll out to ¼-inch thickness. Cut out the cookies using a cutter 1 to 2½ inches in diameter (or whatever shape you like). Repeat with remaining portion of dough. Gather the scraps and reroll until all the dough is used. Place the cookies about 1 inch apart on ungreased baking sheets, and refrigerate for 15 minutes.

Bake the cookies: Heat the oven to 350°F. Sprinkle the cookies with colored sugar or sprinkles if you wish. Bake until firm but not brown—12 to 15 minutes. Cool the cookies on the baking sheets 2 minutes, then transfer to wire racks to cool completely. If you like, you can sandwich the cookies with jam or drizzle them with melted chocolate—or both.

chocolate-covered peanut butter balls

MAKES approximately 60 one-inch balls
WORKING TIME 45 minutes
TOTAL TIME 45 minutes plus cooling

I'm always happy when Teri calls to tell me she's received her holiday box of these sweet treats from her mother-in-law, Sandy. I think you'll agree I'm lucky to have a friend who shares both the cookies and the recipe. SHOWN ON PAGE 74.

2 cups chunky peanut butter
1 cup unsalted butter (2 sticks), softened
4 cups confectioners' sugar
3 cups crisp rice cereal
2 cups dark chocolate chips (12 ounces)
2 tablespoons vegetable shortening
½ cup white chocolate chips (3 ounces)

Make the balls: Line 2 baking sheets with waxed paper and set aside. Cream the peanut butter and butter together in a large bowl with an electric mixer set on medium speed until fluffy—2 to 3 minutes. Add the confectioners' sugar with the mixer on low speed, beating until combined. Stir in the rice cereal with a wooden spoon until fully incorporated. Roll the dough by the tablespoonful between your palms, into balls about 1 inch in diameter. Place on the prepared baking sheets.

Dip the balls: Place the dark chocolate chips and shortening in a small microwave-safe bowl and microwave on high for 30 seconds; remove and stir. If not completely melted, repeat the microwaving. Using a fork, dip each peanut butter ball into the chocolate, coating well and letting the excess drip off. Transfer the balls as they are coated to the prepared baking sheets. Allow to cool until set. To speed up the setting time, you can refrigerate the sheets until the chocolate is hard.

Garnish the balls: Place the white chocolate chips in a small microwave-safe bowl and microwave on medium for 30 seconds; remove and stir. If not completely melted, repeat the microwaving. Pour the melted chocolate into a plastic sandwich bag. Snip off the tip of one corner of the bag with scissors. Drizzle the white chocolate over each peanut butter ball. Let set until firm. Store in an airtight container.

TIP *Many older candy recipes will call for adding paraffin wax to the chocolate. It adds a shiny finish as well as stabilizing the chocolate, preventing fat bloom (when the chocolate turns white). To avoid using wax, consider substituting vegetable shortening or use wax-free chocolate candy melts available at most craft stores or grocery markets during the holiday season.*

snowballs

MAKES 24 one-inch cookies
WORKING TIME 30 minutes
TOTAL TIME 1 hour

This recipe is a traditional holiday favorite of my family that I have been making since I was a little girl. I always bake the first batch of the season the night we decorate our Christmas tree. SHOWN ON PAGE 74.

½ cup unsalted butter (1 stick), softened
2 tablespoons honey
1 teaspoon vanilla extract
1 cup all-purpose flour
1 cup chopped pecans (about 4 ounces)
¾ cup confectioners' sugar

Make the dough: Grease 2 large baking sheets. Heat the oven to 350°F. Beat the butter and honey in a medium-size bowl with an electric mixer on medium speed until well combined and fluffy—2 to 3 minutes. Lower the mixer speed to medium-low and beat in the vanilla; then beat in the flour and pecans until combined.

Shape the dough: Roll the dough by the tablespoonful between your palms, into balls. Place on the prepared baking sheets, spacing 1 inch apart.

Bake the cookies: Bake the cookies just until they turn light golden brown—12 to 14 minutes. Cool on the baking sheets 1 minute, then transfer to wire racks to cool completely.

Garnish the cookies: Put the confectioners' sugar into a large plastic food-storage bag. Add the cookies, 6 at a time, and gently shake the bag until they are coated with sugar.

holiday spritz cookies

MAKES about seventy-two 1½-inch cookies
WORKING TIME 25 minutes
TOTAL TIME 2 hours

I was so excited when I bought my first cookie press at a Goodwill store as a teenager. No Christmas since has been celebrated without my little spritz trees and snowflakes. Not only are they perfectly tiny and buttery, they're just so darn cute! SHOWN ON PAGE 44.

2¼ cups all-purpose flour
¼ teaspoon salt
1 cup unsalted butter (2 sticks), softened
½ cup sugar
1 large egg
1 teaspoon vanilla extract
Colored sprinkles, for topping (optional)

Make the dough: Heat the oven to 375°F. Mix the flour and salt in a small bowl. Cream the butter and sugar in a large bowl with an electric mixer on medium speed until fluffy—2 to 3 minutes. Add the egg and vanilla and beat until smooth. Lower the mixer speed to medium-low and gradually add the flour mixture, beating until smooth.

Shape and bake the cookies: Pack some of the dough into a cookie press fitted with the disk of your choice. Press the cookies directly on ungreased baking sheets, spacing about 1 inch apart, following your cookie press instructions. If you like, top each cookie with colored sprinkles. Bake until the edges are firm and just beginning to turn pale brown—8 to 10 minutes. Cool the cookies on the baking sheets 2 minutes, then transfer to wire racks to cool completely.

The Cookie Press

My mini spritz trees became mini-tree sandwich cookies with frosting in the middle. I tinted some dough green and pressed out tiny wreaths, which I covered with edible metallic balls that felt as if they'd crack your teeth when you bit into them. High production was my goal, and soon the kitchen was covered in cookies. I couldn't help but admire how professional they all looked! Excitedly, I gathered up several pretty old plates and arranged thoughtful assortments of my fancy cookies. I drove to all the neighbors' houses, delivering my special holiday treats and spreading holiday cheer. I always knew the cookie press was going to make my world a better place!

One of my favorite childhood pastimes was reading through old cookbooks, many inherited from my grandmothers, who had both passed away before I was born. I especially loved reading the recipes for baked goods and the pamphlets from companies like Hershey's and Karo. One all-time favorite was a pamphlet that originally came with an old-fashioned cookie press. Although the cookie press was long gone, I loved looking at the photos and admiring all the amazing shapes that the press could create. Being the dreamer that I was, I added a cookie press to my list of dream items I would love to have someday.

Several years later, as a teenager shopping with my mom at Goodwill, I spotted a vintage cookie-press set, complete with the original box. For Christmas that year, I made a double batch of spritz cookie dough and started pressing cookies to my heart's content. I had no idea how many cookies just one batch would make and quickly discovered a double batch was definitely not necessary.

Cookie Tips

DOUGH ROLLING TIPS

★ To begin, sprinkle your work surface, disk of dough, and rolling pin with a little flour. You can roll dough between sheets of waxed paper instead—if the paper crinkles, it's easy to lift off and adjust.

★ If the dough cracks when you roll it, it's probably too cold. Let it sit at room temperature for a few minutes to soften.

★ After cutting as many cookies as you can from the rolled dough, gather the dough scraps, shape them into a fresh disk, and reroll. You can chill the disk again if you like. Cookie dough won't become tough with repeated rolling the way pastry dough does, so it's okay to repeat until all your dough is used.

A COOKIE SCOOP MAKES IT EASY

Cookie scoops are readily available at kitchen stores in a variety of sizes. A 1½-inch scoop holds about 4 teaspoons or a generous tablespoon of dough and works for most cookie recipes. This gadget makes quick work of dropping the dough onto the baking sheet, and has the added benefit of creating uniform cookies.

ABOUT BAKING SHEETS

The type of baking sheet you use affects the way cookies turn out. Heavy-gauge aluminum with a dull finish produces the most evenly browned cookies. Double-thick insulated sheets discourage overbaking (and may increase baking time slightly). Dark baking sheets may cause cookie bottoms to overbrown, so watch closely. Rimless sheets are best because they allow the oven air to circulate efficiently.

COOKIE STORAGE TIPS

★ Be sure your cookies are completely cool before putting them in storage containers.

★ Store each recipe separately so the flavors don't blend and the texture isn't compromised.

★ Store soft cookies at room temperature in a container with a tight lid, or in a resealable food storage bag.

★ Store crisp cookies at room temperature in a container with a loose-fitting lid.

★ Most cookies will keep for up to two weeks at room temperature.

★ If you wish to freeze baked cookies, place in an airtight container, cushioned with crumpled waxed paper. If they've been decorated, first place in a single layer on a baking sheet and freeze; then pack. Or freeze before decorating, and then defrost and decorate right before using.

★ To freeze unbaked cookie dough, tightly wrap first in heavy-duty foil and then in plastic wrap. Thaw in the refrigerator.

COOKIE PACKING TIPS

★ If you're giving cookies to nearby friends, just cushion with crumpled waxed paper or parchment paper and nestle into a pretty container. They'll be eaten too quickly to require you to wrap different types individually!

★ Soft cookies and bars are the best long-distance travelers because they're not prone to breaking, but other types ship well if cushioned properly.

　　★ Line your container with waxed paper, parchment paper, or aluminum foil. Wrap cookies in pairs, airtight in plastic wrap or foil, placing them back-to-back if you can. Wrap balls and bars individually. Then arrange them in the container, adding crumpled waxed or parchment paper or foil as a cushion. Fill the container—you don't want the contents jostling around as they travel. Tape shut if the lid is not absolutely tight.

　　★ Place the container in a sturdy shipping box and cushion it so it fits snugly.

raspberry thumbprints

MAKES about thirty-two 1¾-inch cookies
WORKING TIME 30 minutes
TOTAL TIME 1 hour

I was always convinced that these cookies were Santa's favorite and made sure to leave him a plateful every Christmas Eve. My boys have carried on this tradition. How could Santa, with a belly like jelly, not love these? SHOWN ABOVE.

½ cup plus 3 tablespoons unsalted butter
  (1 stick plus 3 tablespoons), softened
½ cup sugar
2 large eggs, separated
½ teaspoon vanilla extract
1½ cups all-purpose flour
1 cup sweetened shredded coconut or finely
  chopped walnuts
½ cup raspberry jam

Make the dough: Grease 2 large baking sheets and set aside. Cream the butter in a medium-size bowl with an electric mixer on medium speed until smooth—2 to 3 minutes. Add the sugar and beat until fluffy. Add the egg yolks and vanilla, and beat until well combined. Lower the mixer speed to medium-low, beat in the flour, and beat until the dough comes together.

Shape the dough: Heat the oven to 350°F. Lightly beat the egg whites in a shallow bowl. Place the coconut in a shallow dish. Roll the dough by the heaping teaspoonful between your palms, into balls. Using a fork, coat the balls in the egg white, then in the coconut. Place on the prepared baking sheets, spacing 1 inch apart. Using your finger, make a deep indentation in center of each cookie.

Bake the cookies: Bake the cookies until lightly golden brown—approximately 15 to 18 minutes. Cool on the baking sheets 10 minutes, then transfer to wire racks to cool completely.

Fill the cookies: Spoon a little raspberry jam (about 1 teaspoon) into the indentation of each cookie.

TIP *These cookies are best when filled with jam just before serving. You can prepare the cookies in advance and store in an airtight container, and then fill them when ready to serve.*

dark chocolate mint cookies

MAKES about forty 2½-inch cookies
WORKING TIME 25 minutes
TOTAL TIME 55 minutes

Anyone would love to receive these rich, chocolate mint cookies, but you can easily accent the flavor differently by using butterscotch or peanut butter chips instead of mint. Whichever kind of chips you choose, make sure to use Dutch-processed cocoa as it gives an especially rich, deep flavor and color. SHOWN ON PAGE 90.

> 2¼ cups all-purpose flour
> ⅔ cup Dutch-processed cocoa powder
> 1 teaspoon baking soda
> ½ teaspoon salt
> 1 cup unsalted butter (2 sticks), softened
> ⅔ cup granulated sugar
> ⅔ cup brown sugar
> 1 teaspoon vanilla extract
> 2 large eggs
> 1 cup mint-flavored chips (6 ounces)

Make the dough: Heat the oven to 350°F. Whisk together the flour, cocoa powder, baking soda, and salt in a medium-sized bowl. Cream the butter in a large bowl with an electric mixer on medium speed; add the granulated and brown sugars and vanilla, beating until creamy—2 to 3 minutes. Add the eggs to the butter mixture, beating until combined. Lower the mixer speed to medium-low and gradually add the flour mixture, beating until smooth. Stir in the mint chips with a wooden spoon.

Bake the cookies: Using a 1½-inch cookie scoop (or by rounded tablespoonfuls), drop the dough onto baking sheets. Bake until slightly set—9 to 11 minutes; the cookies will appear to be slightly undercooked in the center, but will firm up once they've cooled. Cool on the baking sheets 2 minutes and transfer to wire racks to cool completely. Store in an airtight container.

TIP *Typically, baking cocoa comes out of its container with some lumps—a quick shake through a sieve will remove them.*

toasted almond biscotti

MAKES about forty 2½-inch-long cookies
WORKING TIME 20 minutes
TOTAL TIME 1 hour 30 minutes plus cooling

These biscotti are not too sweet and are perfect for dipping into a hot cup of coffee or cocoa. Packaged in jars or cellophane bags and tied with a ribbon, they make an easy, thoughtful gift. SHOWN ON PAGE 78.

> 1 cup almonds with skins (about 5½ ounces)
> 2 cups all-purpose flour
> 1½ teaspoons baking powder
> ¼ teaspoon salt
> ½ cup unsalted butter (1 stick), softened
> ¾ cup sugar
> 2 large eggs
> 2 teaspoons vanilla extract

Toast the almonds: Heat the oven to 350°F. Coarsely chop the almonds and place on a baking sheet. Bake until golden brown—about 15 minutes. Remove from the oven and let cool. Lower the oven temperature to 325°F.

Make the dough: Combine the flour, baking powder, and salt in a medium-size bowl. Cream the butter and sugar in a large bowl with an electric mixer on medium speed until fluffy—2 to 3 minutes. Beat in the eggs one at a time. Beat in the vanilla. Lower the mixer speed to medium-low and gradually beat in the flour mixture until well combined. Beat in the almonds.

Shape the dough: Transfer the dough to a lightly floured work surface. Using lightly floured hands, divide the dough in half and shape each half into a slightly flattened log about 16 inches long.

Bake the cookies: Place the dough logs on a baking sheet and bake for 25 minutes. Transfer the baking sheet to a wire rack and cool for 10 minutes. Using a serrated bread knife, diagonally cut each log into approximately 20 slices, each ¾ inch thick. Arrange the cookies, cut side down, on the baking sheet. Bake until pale golden—15 to 20 minutes. Remove the baking sheet from oven and turn the cookies over; bake until toasty brown—an additional 15 to 20 minutes. Transfer the cookies to a wire rack to cool.

TIP *For a sweet indulgence, dip the end of each cooled biscotti into melted chocolate. Cool on waxed paper and refrigerate until set.*

chocolate-drizzled almond macaroons

MAKES about 36 two-inch cookies
WORKING TIME 15 minutes
TOTAL TIME 1 hour 30 minutes

If you like Almond Joy candy bars, you'll love these moist-on-the-inside and crunchy-on-the-outside macaroons. Toasting the almonds not only brings out their flavor, it adds an extra crunch. Plus, the dark chocolate drizzle makes these treats look as good as they taste. SHOWN ON PAGE 64.

  1 cup blanched almonds (5½ ounces), coarsely chopped
5⅓ cups sweetened flaked coconut (14 ounces)
  3 tablespoons all-purpose flour
  ¼ teaspoon salt
  1 14-ounce can sweetened condensed milk
  2 large egg whites, at room temperature
  1 teaspoon vanilla extract
  ¼ teaspoon almond extract
  1 cup dark or semisweet chocolate chips (6 ounces)

Toast the almonds: Heat oven to 350°F. Toast the almonds on a baking sheet for about 8 minutes, or until fragrant. Transfer to a plate to cool; then finely chop. Leave the oven on.

Make the batter: Lightly butter 3 baking sheets. Whisk together the flour, salt, and coconut in a large bowl. Add the condensed milk, mixing until combined. Using an electric mixer on high speed, beat the egg whites and vanilla and almond extracts in a large bowl until stiff peaks form. Fold the egg white mixture into the coconut mixture. Gently stir in the almonds.

Bake the cookies: Using a 1½-inch cookie scoop (or by rounded tablespoonfuls), drop the batter onto the prepared baking sheets. Bake until firm—22 to 24 minutes. Transfer the cookies from the baking sheets to a wire rack to cool.

Drizzle cookies with chocolate: Place the chocolate chips in a small microwave-safe bowl and microwave on high for 30 seconds; remove and stir. If not completely melted, repeat the microwaving. Stir until smooth and slightly cooled. Pour into a plastic sandwich bag. Use scissors to snip off the tip of one corner and then drizzle the chocolate over the top of the cooled cookies. Store in an airtight container.

TIP *To prevent the bottoms of the cookies from browning, place parchment paper on baking sheets instead of lightly buttering. This makes cleanup much easier too!*

holiday spice logs

MAKES 72 two-inch cookies
WORKING TIME 30 minutes
TOTAL TIME 1 hour 50 minutes

These tiny little spice cookies have the added goodness of chocolate, and dipping them in red and green jimmies makes them so colorful and perfect for gift-giving. SHOWN ON PAGE 64.

2¾ cups all-purpose flour
1 teaspoon ground nutmeg
1 teaspoon ground cinnamon
¼ teaspoon salt
1 cup unsalted butter (2 sticks), softened
1 cup sugar
2 teaspoons vanilla extract
1 large egg
1 cup semisweet chocolate chips
  Multi-colored jimmies (sprinkles)

Make the dough: Heat the oven to 350°F. Whisk the flour, nutmeg, cinnamon, and salt together in a medium-size bowl. Cream the butter and sugar in a large bowl with an electric mixer on medium-low speed until smooth—2 to 3 minutes. Add the vanilla and egg, beating until well combined. Gradually add the flour mixture, beating until fully incorporated.

Shape the dough: Divide the dough in half and slice each half into six sections. Work with one section at a time, keeping the others covered with plastic wrap. Roll each section into a 12-inch-long log about ½ inch in diameter. Slice the log into 2-inch-long pieces and place on a baking sheet. Repeat with remaining dough.

Bake the cookies: Bake the cookies until set—12 to 14 minutes. Cool the cookies on the baking sheets 2 minutes and transfer to wire racks to cool completely.

Garnish the ends: Place the chocolate chips in a small microwave-safe bowl and microwave on high for 30 seconds; remove and stir. If not completely melted, repeat the microwaving. Stir until smooth. Place the jimmies in a small, shallow bowl. Dip one end of each cookie first into the melted chocolate and then into the jimmies. Place the dipped cookies on waxed paper and let sit until the chocolate is cool and firm.

mini meringue stars

MAKES 200 dime-sized meringues
WORKING TIME 20 minutes
TOTAL TIME 1 hour 20 minutes

I love all things miniature and decided I could take a standard meringue cookie and make it special by shrinking it down. The result is a teeny delicious bite that's perfect to pack 10, 20, or 30 at a time for gifts.
SHOWN ABOVE RIGHT.

  2 large egg whites, at room temperature
½ teaspoon vanilla extract
¼ teaspoon cream of tartar
⅔ cup granulated or superfine sugar

Make the meringues: Heat the oven to 300°F. Line 3 to 4 large baking sheets with parchment paper. Beat the egg whites, vanilla, and cream of tartar in a medium-size bowl with an electric mixer on high speed until frothy. Slowly add the sugar, continuing to beat on high speed until the mixture forms very stiff peaks.

Bake the meringues: Fit a large pastry bag with a star tip (a #21 tip works well). Add the meringue mixture to the bag. Dab some meringue under the corners of the parchment on baking sheets to secure the paper to the sheets. Pipe tiny (dime-size) meringues onto the prepared baking sheets, spacing about ½ inch apart. Bake just until the meringues begin to brown very slightly and are firm to the touch—12 to 14 minutes. Cool on the baking sheets on wire racks. Store in an airtight container.

tiny lemon meringue tarts

MAKES twenty-four 1¾-inch tarts
WORKING TIME 1 hour
TOTAL TIME 1 hour 15 minutes plus cooling

I love how fancy these tiny lemon meringue tarts look, and they're equally tasty. I prefer to serve them the day they're prepared, when the meringue is perfectly crisped on the outside—it loses that crispy appeal if it sits overnight. Whenever I make these, I get lots of oohs and aahs. SHOWN ON PAGE 76.

½ cup plus 1 tablespoon unsalted butter
    (1 stick plus 1 tablespoon), softened
2 ounces cream cheese, softened
1 cup all-purpose flour
1½ teaspoons finely grated lemon zest
⅓ cup sugar
1 tablespoon cornstarch
⅓ cup cold water
1 large egg yolk
2 tablespoons freshly squeezed lemon juice
1 recipe meringue (recipe follows)

Make the crust: Heat the oven to 325°F. Lightly grease a 24-cup mini-muffin pan and set it aside. Beat ½ cup butter and the cream cheese in a small bowl with an electric mixer on medium speed until smooth—2 minutes. Lower the mixer speed to medium-low and add the flour and 1 teaspoon of the lemon zest, beating until the mixture comes together in a ball. Roll the dough by the heaping teaspoonful between your palms, into 24 balls. Press each ball into the bottom and up the sides of the prepared pan. Bake the shells until lightly browned on the inside—approximately 20 minutes. Meanwhile, make the lemon filling.

Make the filling: Combine the sugar, cornstarch, water, egg yolk, remaining ½ teaspoon grated lemon zest, and lemon juice in a medium-size saucepan, whisking together until the cornstarch is completely dissolved. Cook on medium-high heat until the mixture begins to bubble and thicken, whisking continually. Cook for 1 minute more, continuing to whisk. Remove from the heat and whisk in the remaining 1 tablespoon butter until melted and the mixture is smooth.

Bake the tarts: Place the pan with the tart shells on a wire rack and let cool. Increase the oven temperature to 350°F. Make the meringue. Spoon the filling into the tart shells, dividing evenly, and top each with meringue. Bake until the meringue is lightly browned—approximately 7 minutes. Cool in the pan on a wire rack. When cool, run a knife around outside edges of the tarts and remove them from the pan.

Meringue

Place 2 large room-temperature egg whites, ½ teaspoon vanilla extract, and ½ teaspoon cream of tartar in a small mixing bowl. Beat with an electric mixer on high speed until the mixture is very frothy. Slowly add 5 tablespoons sugar, continuing to beat on high until the mixture forms stiff peaks.

TIP *Topping the tarts is easy if you spoon the meringue into a pastry bag or a plastic food storage bag with one corner snipped off, and then pipe it over the tarts.*

metric equivalent charts

The recipes in this book use the standard United States method for measuring liquid and dry or solid ingredients (teaspoons, tablespoons, and cups). The information on this chart is provided to help cooks outside the U.S. successfully use these recipes. All equivalents are approximate.

METRIC EQUIVALENTS FOR DIFFERENT TYPES OF INGREDIENTS
A standard cup measure of a dry or solid ingredient will vary in weight depending on the type of ingredient. A standard cup of liquid is the same volume for any type of liquid. Use the following chart when converting standard cup measures to grams (weight) or milliliters (volume).

STANDARD CUP	FINE POWDER (E.G., FLOUR)	GRAIN (E.G., RICE)	GRANULAR (E.G., SUGAR)	LIQUID SOLIDS (E.G., BUTTER)	LIQUID (E.G., MILK)
1	140 g	150 g	190 g	200 g	240 ml
¾	105 g	113 g	143 g	150 g	180 ml
⅔	93 g	100 g	125 g	133 g	160 ml
½	70 g	75 g	95 g	100 g	120 ml
⅓	47 g	50 g	63 g	67 g	80 ml
¼	35 g	38 g	48 g	50 g	60 ml
⅛	18 g	19 g	24 g	25 g	30 ml

USEFUL EQUIVALENTS FOR LIQUID INGREDIENTS BY VOLUME

¼ tsp	=					1 ml
½ tsp	=					2 ml
1 tsp	=					5 ml
3 tsp	=	1 tblsp	=		½ fl oz =	15 ml
		2 tblsp	=	⅛ cup =	1 fl oz =	30 ml
		4 tblsp	=	¼ cup =	2 fl oz =	60 ml
		5⅓ tblsp	=	⅓ cup =	3 fl oz =	80 ml
		8 tblsp	=	½ cup =	4 fl oz =	120 ml
		10⅔ tblsp	=	⅔ cup =	5 fl oz =	160 ml
		12 tblsp	=	¾ cup =	6 fl oz =	180 ml
		16 tblsp	=	1 cup =	8 fl oz =	240 ml
		1 pt	=	2 cups =	16 fl oz =	480 ml
		1 qt	=	4 cups =	32 fl oz =	960 ml
					33 fl oz =	1000 ml = 1 l

USEFUL EQUIVALENTS FOR DRY INGREDIENTS BY WEIGHT
(To convert ounces to grams, multiply the number of ounces by 30.)

1 oz	=	¹⁄₁₆ lb	=	30 g
4 oz	=	¼ lb	=	120 g
8 oz	=	½ lb	=	240 g
12 oz	=	¾ lb	=	360 g
16 oz	=	1 lb	=	480 g

USEFUL EQUIVALENTS FOR COOKING/OVEN TEMPERATURES

	FARENHEIT	CELCIUS	GAS MARK
Freeze Water	32° F	0° C	
Room Temperature	68° F	20° C	
Boil Water	212° F	100° C	
Bake	325° F	160° C	3
	350° F	180° C	4
	375° F	190° C	5
	400° F	200° C	6
	425° F	220° C	7
	450° F	23° C	8
Broil			Grill

USEFUL EQUIVALENTS FOR LENGTH
(To convert inches to centimeters, multiply the number of inches by 2.5)

1 in	=					2.5 cm	
6 in	=	½ ft	=			15 cm	
12 in	=	1 ft	=			30 cm	
36 in	=	3 ft	=	1 yd	=	90 cm	
40 in	=					100 cm	= 1 m

index

www.thefarmchicks.com

PHOTOGRAPHY CREDITS
All photography by John Granen with the following exceptions:
iStockphoto: 22 (ornament), 33 (reindeer), 49 (bell), 81 (ornaments), 115, 117; Philip Dyer: 16 (snowflake); Jill Fromer: 23 (ornaments); Francesco Rossetti: 48-53, 90-93, 104-109 (clothespins); Stefan Klein: 63 (mistletoe); Lisa Thornberg: 66 (stars); Cheryl Graham: 71 middle left; Fielding Peipereit: 86 (star); Thomas Milewski: 93 bottom left; Olga Drozdova: 96 (mittens); Gary Martin: 101 (pine cone); Ann Cady: 102 (gum drops); Ivonne Wierink-vanWetten: 111; James Knighten: 113; Lauri Patterson: 120; Alina Solovyova-Vincent: 122
Debra McClinton: 53 (all photos)
Shutterstock: 4, 5, 25, 30 (pine needles); Cindy Hughes: 21 (lights); Leach: 34, 42, 58, 68, 80 (lights); Deborah Cloyed: 48, 50, 52, 90, 92, 104, 106, 108 (stocking); Andy Platt: 83 (peppermint); Ronald van der Beek: 107 (candy cane)
Courtesy of Serena Thompson: 18

The Farm Chicks gift tags, labels, and recipe cards were designed by Elle Price, www.shopellesstudio.com
Sticker and note card designs were adapted for inclusion by woolypear

Project Editor: Carol Spier
Design: woolypear

Library of Congress Cataloging-in-Publication Data

Thompson, Serena.
   The Farm Chicks Christmas : merry ideas for the holidays / Serena
Thompson.
       p. cm.
   Includes index.
   ISBN 978-1-58816-521-3
   1. Christmas decorations. 2. Christmas cookery. I. Title.
   TT900.C4T487 2010
   745.594'12--dc22
                                    2010004092

10 9 8 7 6 5 4 3 2 1

Published by Hearst Books
A division of Sterling Publishing Co., Inc.
387 Park Avenue South, New York, NY 10016

The Farm Chicks is a trademark of The Farm Chicks, Inc.
Country Living is a registered trademark of Hearst Communications, Inc.

www.countryliving.com

For information about custom editions, special sales, premium and corporate purchases, please contact Sterling Special Sales Department at 800-805-5489 or specialsales@sterlingpublishing.com.

Distributed in Canada by Sterling Publishing
C/o Canadian Manda Group, 165 Dufferin Street
Toronto, Ontario, Canada M6K 3H6

Distributed in Australia by Capricorn Link (Australia) Pty. Ltd.
P.O. Box 704, Windsor, NSW 2756 Australia

Manufactured in China

Sterling ISBN 978-1-58816-521-3

to:

from:

Baked for you by:

Merry Christmas!

to:

from:

Baked for you by:

Recipe:
....
....
....
....
....
....
....
....

★ FARM CHICKS

....
....
....
....
....
....
....

Recipe:
....
....
....
....
....
....
....
....
....

★ FARM CHICKS

Recipe:
....
....
....
....
....
....
....
....
....
....

★ FARM CHICKS

to:

from:

Baked for you by:

Merry
Christmas!

to:

from:

Baked for you by:

Recipe:

....
....
....
....
....
....
....
....
....

THE ★ FARM CHICKS

....
....
....
....
....
....
....
....

Recipe:

....
....
....
....
....
....
....
....
....
....

THE ★ FARM CHICKS

Recipe:

....
....
....
....
....
....
....
....
....
....
....

THE ★ FARM CHICKS

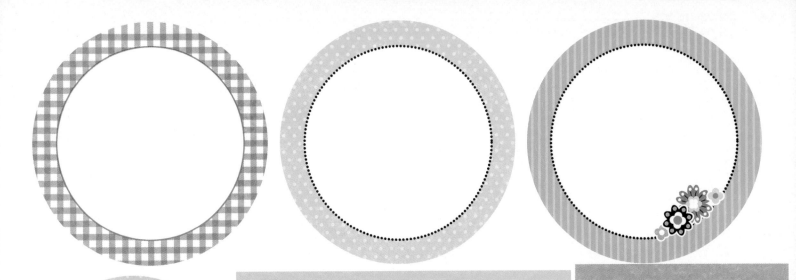

From our
house
to yours!

Merry
Christmas!

— Note —

Baked
for you
with love

Baked for you by:

to

from

to

from

to

from

to

from

to

from

Merry Christmas!

to: from:

merry christmas

Baked with love

by:

Merry Christmas

to:

from:

Baked for you by:

Merry Christmas!

Farm Chicks
Note Cards

Here are eight cute cards to use for greetings, gift tags, or even invitations. Detach the cards along the perfo-rations. Add a message or short recipe to the back as indicated, and send the card to someone special or tuck it into a gift. If you're giving homemade cookies to a loved one, your gift will be even more meaningful if the recipe is included— that way the recipient will be able to enjoy the cookies again and again.